Doris Lessing

A Checklist of

Primary and Secondary Sources

Doris Lessing

A Checklist of
Primary and Secondary Sources

by

Selma R. Burkom

with

Margaret Williams

The Whitston Publishing Company
Incorporated
Troy New York
1973

Copyright 1973
Selma R. Burkom

Library of Congress Catalog Card Number: 72–87109

ISBN 0–87875–039–8

Printed in the United States of America

INTRODUCTION

This checklist enumerates the basic editions of Doris Lessing's works and the critical responses they have elicited. The catalog of secondary materials makes no claim to being exhaustive: no chronicler can keep up with the mass of Lessing criticism which has begun appearing recently. Hopefully, the most important pieces written to date have been included.

The checklist has three parts. In part I, primary sources, Lessing's publications are divided into four sections: (A) books and pamphlets; (B) contributions to books; (C) contributions to periodicals; (D) translations. Sections A, B and C are chronologically ordered by the publication dates of the listed materials. Section D is alphabetized according to the name of the country in which the translation was published.

In part II, secondary sources, the criticism of Lessing's work is divided into four sections: (E) interviews; (F) biography; (G) bibliography; (H) general critiques--*i.e.*, those concerned with more than a single work; (I) critiques of individual works. All sections are alphabetized according to the authors' names.

The checklist concludes with an index in which all of Lessing's titles and the names of all of her critics are alphabetized. Here, the letters and numbers refer to the upper case and arabic symbols which identify the items and run consecutively through parts I and II.

Several formal practices need mention. Easily recognizable shortened forms have been used for the names of magazines and publishers. Additionally, there are two letter abbreviations. "NY" is used for "New York" in all instances; e.g., "NY Times" refers to the [daily] "New York Times." "NYTBR" refers to the [Sunday] "New York Times Book Review" [magazine]. Finally, two sorts of emendations are enclosed in square brackets. First, when the genre of a Lessing work is not clear, it is given following the title. Second, for all translations, the foreign title is followed by the original source of the material.

It will be noted that several items are not complete. These are entries which I have been unable to personally verify. They were cited in Dorothy Brewster's *Doris Lessing* (Twayne, 1965); I include them out of respect for that writer's scholarship.

I should like to acknowledge my debt not only to Brewster's book but also to Catharina Ipp's *Doris Lessing: A Bibliography* (Johannesburg, 1962). My undertaking owes much to these earlier works. I should like to express my appreciation to the reference staffs of the libraries at Stanford University and Dominican College of San Rafael. Their aid was immeasurable. Thanks are due for a grant and a leave-of-absence from Kirkland College.

Selma R. Burkom

CONTENTS

I. WORKS BY LESSING

II. CRITICISM OF LESSING'S WORKS

CONTENTS CON'T.

I. WORKS BY LESSING

A. BOOKS AND PAMPHLETS

1. THE GRASS IS SINGING [novel].

    London: Michael Joseph, 1950.
    New York: Crowell, 1950.

2. THIS WAS THE OLD CHIEF'S COUNTRY: STORIES.

    London: Michael Joseph, 1951.
    New York: Crowell, 1952.

    Contents: The old chief Mshlanga--A sunrise on
    the veld--No witchcraft for sale--The second hut--
    The nuisance--The De Wets come to Kloof Grange--
    Little Tembi--Old John's place--'Leopard' George--
    Winter in July

3. MARTHA QUEST [novel].

    London: Michael Joseph, 1952.

    Bk. I of the series CHILDREN OF VIOLENCE; see
    A.28.

4.   FIVE: SHORT NOVELS.

       London: Michael Joseph, 1953.

         Contents: A home for the highland cattle--The other woman--Eldorado--The antheap--Hunger

5.   A PROPER MARRIAGE [novel].

       London: Michael Joseph, 1954.

       Bk. II of the series CHILDREN OF VIOLENCE; see A.28.

6.   RETREAT TO INNOCENCE [novel].

       London: Michael Joseph, 1956.

7.   NO WITCHCRAFT FOR SALE: STORIES AND SHORT NOVELS.

       Moscow: Foreign Languages Publishing House, 1956.

         Contents: The old chief Mshlanga--No witchcraft for sale--The nuisance--Little Tembi--'Leopard' George--The antheap--Hunger

8.   THE HABIT OF LOVING [short stories].

       London: MacGibbon and Kee, 1957.
       New York: Crowell, 1958.

         Contents: The habit of loving--The words he said--The woman--Through the tunnel--Lucy Grange--

Pleasure--A mild attack of locusts--The witness--
Flavours of exile--Flight--The day Stalin died--
Plants and girls--Wine--He--The eye of God in
paradise

9. GOING HOME: DRAWINGS BY PAUL HOGARTH
   [personal narrative].

   London: Michael Joseph, 1957.

10. MR. DOLLINGER [play].

    Unpublished; produced at the Oxford Playhouse, Eng-
    land, 1958.

11. A RIPPLE FROM THE STORM [novel].

    London: Michael Joseph, 1958.

    Bk. III of the series CHILDREN OF VIOLENCE;
    see A.28.

12. EACH HIS OWN WILDERNESS [play].

    Produced by the English Stage Society at the Royal
    Court Theatre, London, 1958; for published script see
    B.32.

13. FOURTEEN POEMS.

    Northwood (England): Scorpion Press, 1959.

Contents: 'Under a low sky'--Older woman to
younger man (1)--Older woman to younger man
(2)--Plea for the hated dead woman--Bars--Dark
girl's song--New man--Night-talk--Song--Exiles--
Oh cherry trees you are too white for my heart--
Fable--In time of dryness--Jealousy

14.   IN PURSUIT OF THE ENGLISH: A DOCUMENTARY.

London: MacGibbon and Kee, 1960.
New York: Simon and Schuster, 1961.

15.   THE TRUTH ABOUT BILLY NEWTON [play].

Unpublished; produced in Salisbury, England, 1961.

16.   THE GOLDEN NOTEBOOK [novel].

London: Michael Joseph, 1962.
New York: Simon and Schuster, 1962.

17.   PLAY WITH A TIGER: A PLAY IN THREE ACTS.

London: Michael Joseph, 1962.

First produced at the Comedy Theatre, London, 1962.

18.   A MAN AND TWO WOMEN [short stories].

London: MacGibbon and Kee, 1963.
New York: Simon and Schuster, 1963.

Contents: One off the short list--The story of

two dogs--The sun between their feet--A woman
on a roof--How I finally lost my heart--A man and
two women--A room--England versus England--Two
potters--Between men--A letter from home--Our
friend Judith--Each other--Homage for Isaac Babel-
Outside the ministry--Dialogue--Notes for a case
history--The new man--To room nineteen

19.   AFRICAN STORIES

London: Michael Joseph, 1964.
New York: Simon and Schuster, 1965.

Contents: The black madonna--The trinket box--
The pig--Traitors--The old chief Mshlanga--A sunrise on the veld--No witchcraft for sale--The second hut--The nuisance--The De Wets come to
Kloof Grange--Little Tembi--Old John's place--
'Leopard' George--Winter in July--A home for the
highland cattle--Eldorado--The antheap--Hunger

20.   LANDLOCKED [novel].

London: MacGibbon and Kee, 1965.

Bk. IV of the series CHILDREN OF VIOLENCE;
see A.28.

21.   BLACK AND WHITE IN AFRICA: THREE STORIES.

Edited and annotated by Kurt Schrey.
Frankfurt: Moritz Diesterweg, 1965.

Contents: The old chief Mshlanga--No witchcraft

Doris Lessing

for sale--Little Tembi

22.   WINTER IN JULY [short stories].

London: Panther, 1966.

> Contents: The second hut--The nuisance--The De Wets come to Kloof Grange--Little Tembi--Old John's place--'Leopard' George--Winter in July

23.   THE BLACK MADONNA [short stories].

London: Panther, 1966.

> Contents: The black madonna--The trinket box--The pig-- Traitors--The old chief Mshlanga--A sunrise on the veld-- No witchcraft for sale

24.   PARTICULARLY CATS [personal narrative].

London: Michael Joseph, 1967.
New York: Simon and Schuster, 1967.

25.   NINE AFRICAN STORIES: WITH A SPECIALLY WRITTEN INTRODUCTION BY THE AUTHOR.

Selected by Michael Marland.
London: Longmans, 1968.

> Contents: No witchcraft for sale--The old chief Mshlanga--A sunrise on the veld--Little Tembi-- The nuisance--A home for the highland cattle-- The second hut--The pig--The antheap

26.   THE FOUR-GATED CITY [novel].

        London: MacGibbon and Kee, 1969.
        New York: Knopf, 1969.

        Bk. V of the series CHILDREN OF VIOLENCE; see
        A.28.

27.   BRIEFING FOR A DESCENT INTO HELL [novel].

        London: Cape, 1971.
        New York: Knopf, 1971.

28.   CHILDREN OF VIOLENCE [a series consisting of
        five linked novels].

        Individual titles and publication dates of the books
        comprising the series:
          Bk. I   MARTHA QUEST (1952)
          Bk. II   A PROPER MARRIAGE (1954)
          Bk. III   A RIPPLE FROM THE STORM (1958)
          Bk. IV   LANDLOCKED (1965)
          Bk. V   THE FOUR-GATED CITY (1969)

        Bks. I and II bound as a single volume: CHILDREN
        OF VIOLENCE.

        New York: Simon and Schuster, 1964.
        London: MacGibbon and Kee, 1965.

        Bks. III and IV bound as a single volume: CHILD-
        REN OF VIOLENCE.

Doris Lessing

London: MacGibbon and Kee, 1965.
New York: Simon and Schuster, 1966.

B. CONTRIBUTIONS TO BOOKS

29.   "The nuisance" [short story]. TOWARDS THE SUN:
       A MISCELLANY OF SOUTHERN AFRICA, ed. Roy
       Macnab. London: Collins, 1950, pp. 29-35.

30.   "The black madonna" [short story]. WINTER'S
       TALES 3. London: Macmillan, 1957, pp. 132-156.

31.   "The small personal voice" [essay]. DECLARA-
       TION, ed. Tom Maschler. London: MacGibbon and
       Kee, 1957, pp. 11-27.

32.   "Each his own wilderness." NEW ENGLISH DRAMA-
       TISTS: THREE PLAYS, ed. E. Martin Browne.
       Harmondsworth: Penguin, 1959, pp. 11-95.

33.   "The De Wets come to Kloof Grange." SOUTH
       AFRICAN STORIES, ed. David Wright. London:
       Farber and Farber, 1960, pp. 98-126.

34. "In pursuit of the English" [excerpt from documentary]. ALIENATION, ed. Timothy O'Keefe. London: MacGibbon and Kee, 1960, pp. 23-50.

35. "Through the tunnel." GREAT STORIES FROM THE WORLD OF SPORT, eds. Peter Schwed and Herbert Warren Wind. London: Heineman, 1960, pp. 130-138.

36. "Flight." SHORT STORIES FROM SOUTHERN AFRICA, ed. A. G. Hooper. Cape Town: Oxford University Press, 1963, pp. 85-90.

37. "A mild attack of locusts." SHORT STORIES FROM SOUTHERN AFRICA, ed. A. G. Hooper. Cape Town: Oxford University Press, 1963, pp. 91-98.

38. "Mrs. Fortescue" [short story]. WINTER'S TALES 9. London: Macmillan, 1963, pp. 149-169.

39. "A sunrise on the veld." SIXTEEN STORIES BY SOUTH AFRICAN WRITERS, ed. Clive Millar. Cape Town: Maskew Miller, 1964, pp. 1-10.

40. "Through the tunnel." SIXTEEN STORIES BY SOUTH AFRICAN WRITERS, ed. Clive Millar. Cape Town: Maskew Miller, 1964, pp. 123-133.

41. "An unposted love letter" [short story]. THY NEIGHBOR'S WIFE: TWELVE ORIGINAL VARIATIONS ON A THEME, ed. James Turner. London: Cassel, 1964, pp. 81-91.

42. "Little Tembi" [short story]. MODERN CHOICE I, ed. Eva Figes. London: Blackie, 1965, pp. 61-94.

43. "To room nineteen" [short story]. THE WORLD OF MODERN FICTION: EUROPEAN, ed. Stephen Marcus. New York: Simon and Schuster, 1966. II, 262-291.

44. "Through the tunnel." BREATH OF DANGER: FIFTY TALES OF PERIL AND FEAR BY MASTERS OF THE SHORT STORY, ed. Eric Duthie. London: Odhams, 1967, pp. 296-305.

45. "Afterword" [essay]. STORY OF AN AFRICAN FARM, Olive Schreiner. Connecticut: Fawcett, 1968, pp. 273-290.

46. "The antheap." GREAT BRITISH SHORT NOVELS, ed. R. D. Spector. New York: Bantam, 1971, pp. 129-183.

47. "An old woman and her cat" [short story]. NEW AMERICAN REVIEW 14, ed. Theodore Solotaroff.

Doris Lessing

New York: Simon and Schuster, 1972, pp. 68-84.

C. CONTRIBUTIONS TO PERIODICALS

48.   "The pig" [short story]. TREK, 12 (April 1948), 16-17.

49.   "Flight" [short story]. TREK, 12 (September 1948), 14-15.

50.   "Under my hand" [poem]. TREK, 13 (February 1949), 25.

51.   "Fruit from ashes" [short story]. TREK, 13 (October 1949), 14-15.

52.   "A mild attack of locusts" [short story]. NEW YORKER, 31 (February 26, 1955), 76-83.

53.   "Through the tunnel" [short story]. NEW YORKER, 31 (August 6, 1955), 60-70.

Doris Lessing

54. "Myself as spokesman" [essay]. NEW YORKER,
31 (January 21, 1956), 78-82.

55. "Being prohibited" [essay]. NEW STATESMAN
AND NATION, 51 (April 2, 1956), 410-412.

56. "Kariba project" [essay]. NEW STATESMAN
AND NATION, 51 (June 9, 1956), 647.

57. "Plea for the hated dead woman" [poem]. NEW
STATESMAN AND NATION, 51 (June 30, 1956),
768.

58. "London diary" [essay]. NEW STATESMAN, 55
(March 15, 1958), 326-327.

59. "London diary" [essay]. NEW STATESMAN,
55 (March 22, 1958), 367-368.

60. "Desert child" [essay]. NEW STATESMAN,
56 (November 15, 1958), 700.

61. "Crisis in central Africa" [essay]. TWENTIETH
CENTURY, 165 (April 1959), 368-376.

62. "Ordinary people" [essay]. NEW STATESMAN,

59 (June 25, 1960), 932.

63. "Our friend Judith" [short story]. PARTISAN
     REVIEW, 27 (Summer 1960), 459-479.

64. "African interiors" [essay]. NEW STATESMAN,
     62 (October 27, 1961), 613-614.

65. "Letter to the editor." NEW STATESMAN, 62
     (November 3, 1961), 651.

66. "Smart set socialists" [essay]. NEW STATESMAN,
     62 (December 1, 1961), 822-824.

67. "Homage for Isaac Babel" [short story]. NEW
     STATESMAN, 62 (December 15, 1961), 920-922.

68. "From the black notebook" [excerpt from THE
     GOLDEN NOTEBOOK]. PARTISAN REVIEW, 29
     (Spring 1962), 196-214.

69. "The new man" [short story]. NEW STATESMAN,
     64 (September 7, 1962), 282-283.

70. "One off the short list" [short story]. KENYON
     REVIEW, 25 (Spring 1963), 217-244.

71.   "A letter from home" [short story]. PARTISAN REVIEW, 30 (Summer 1963), 192-201.

72.   "A room [short story]. NEW STATESMAN, 66 (August 2, 1963), 138-139.

73.   "What really matters" [essay]. TWENTIETH CENTURY, 172 (Autumn 1963), 97-98.

74.   "All seething underneath" [excerpt from IN PURSUIT OF THE ENGLISH]. VOGUE, 143 (February 15, 1964), 80-81, 132-133.

75.   "An elephant in the dark " [essay]. SPECTATOR, 213 (September 18, 1964), 373.

76.   "Zambia's joyful week" [essay]. NEW STATES-MAN, 68 (November 6, 1964), 692-694.

77.   "Allah be praised" [essay]. NEW STATESMAN, 71 (May 27, 1966), 775-779.

78.   "Here" [poem]. NEW STATESMAN, 71 (June 17, 1966), 900.

79.   "Visit" [poem]. NEW STATESMAN, 72 (November 4, 1966), 666.

80. "Particularly cats" [excerpt from personal narrative]. McCALLS, 94 (March 1967), 110-111.

81. "A small girl throws stones at a swan in Regents Park" [poem]. NEW STATESMAN, 74 (November 24, 1967), 731.

82. "Hunger the king" [poem]. NEW STATESMAN, 74 (November 24, 1967), 731.

83. "Omar Khayyam" [essay]. NEW STATESMAN, 74 (December 15, 1967), 847.

84. "Side benefits of an honorable profession" [short story]. PARTISAN REVIEW, 35 (Fall 1968), 507-518.

85. "Particularly cats" [excerpt from personal narrative]. CAT FANCY, 12 (March-April 1969), 49-56.

86. "Particularly cats" (excerpt from the personal narrative). CAT FANCY, 12 (June 1969), 48-56.

87. "A few doors down" [essay]. NEW STATESMAN, 78 (December 26, 1969), 918-919.

Doris Lessing

88. "Report on the threatened city" [short story]. PLAYBOY, 17 (November 1971), 108-10, 250-254, 256, 258, 260, 262.

89. "Spies I have known" [short story]. PARTISAN REVIEW, 38 (Winter 1971), 50-66.

90. "Ancient way to new freedom" [essay]. VOGUE, 158 (July 1971), 98, 125, 130-131.

91. "What looks like an egg and is an egg?" [essay]. NEW YORK TIMES BOOK REVIEW, 77 (May 7, 1972), 6, 41-43.

D. TRANSLATIONS

Belgium

92. HET ZINGENDE GRAS [The Grass Is Singing].

Trans. Paul van Kampen.
Antwerp: Martens and Stappaerts, 1953.

Chile

93. REGRESO A LA INOCENCIA [Retreat to Innocence].

Trans. Cármen Cienfuegos.
Santiago: Zig-Zag, 1969.

Czechoslovakia

94. AFRICKÉ POVÍDKY [stories from This Was the
Old Chief's Country and The Habit of Loving].

Trans. Petr Pujman.
Prague: Statni Nakladatelstvi Krasne Literatury
a Umeni, 1961.

Contents: The old chief Mshlanga--A sunrise on
the veld--No witchcraft for sale--The second hut--

19

The nuisance--Little Tembi--The words he said--
A mild attack of locusts--The witness--Getting
off the altitude--A road to the big city

95. MRAVENIŠTĚ [stories from Five and the Habit of
     Loving].

     Trans. Olga Fialová, Wanda Zámecká, Zora Wolfová.
     Prague: Mlada Fronta, 1961.

     Contents: A home for the highland cattle--The
     other woman--Eldorado--The antheap--Hunger--
     The eye of God in paradise

96. HRA S. TYGREM [Play with a Tiger].

     Trans. Jiří Mucha.
     Prague: Dilia, 1966.

97. MUŽ A DVĚ ŽENY [stories from A Man and Two
     Women].

     Trans. Zora Wolfová.
     Prague: Mlada Fronta, 1970.

     Contents: One off the short list--A woman on a
     roof--How I finally lost my heart--A man and two
     women--England versus England--Two potters--
     Between men--Dialogue--Notes for a case history --
     To room nineteen

A Checklist

Denmark

98. GRAESSET SYNGER [The Grass Is Singing].

Trans. Hagmund Hansen.
Copenhagen: Tremad, 1952.

99. VINTER I JULI [This Was the Old Chief's
Country].

Trans. Hedda Løvlad.
Copenhagen: Aschehoug, 1957.

Contents: The old chief Mshlanga--A sunrise on
the veld--No witchcraft for sale--The second hut--
The nuisance--The De Wets come to Kloof Grange--
Little Tembi--Old John's place--'Leopard' George --
Winter in July

Finland

100. KULTAINEN MUISTRIKIRJA [The Golden Notebook].

Trans. Eeva Siikarla.
Helsinki: Werner Söderström, 1968.

France

101. VAINCUE PAR LA BROUSSE [The Grass Is Singing].

Trans. Doussia Ergaz.
Paris: Plon, 1953.

21

102. LES ENFANTS DE LA VIOLENCE (1): MARTHA QUEST [Children of Violence (1): Martha Quest].

    Trans. Doussia Ergaz and Florence Cravoisier.
    Paris: Plon, 1957.

103. "SA PETITE VOIX PERSONNELLE," en Les Jeunes Gens en Colere vous Parlent ["A Small Personal Voice," in Declaration], pp. 7-30.

    Trans. Michel Chrestien.
    Paris: P. Horay, 1958.

104. UN HOMME, DEUX FEMMES [stories from A Man and Two Women].

    Trans. Jacqueline Marc-Chadourne.
    Paris: Plon, 1967.

    Contents: One off the short list--A woman on a roof--How I finally lost my heart--A man and two women--England versus England--Two potters--Between men--Dialogue--Notes for a case history--To room nineteen

Germany

105. AFRIKANISCHE TRAGÖDIE [The Grass Is Singing].

    Trans. Ernst Sander.
    Gütersloh: Bertelsmann, 1953.

106. DIE ANDERE FRAU ["The Other Woman"].

Trans. Ernst Sander.
Gutersloh: Bertelsmann, 1954.

107. DER ZAUBER IST NICHT VERKÄUFLICH
[stories from Five and This Was the Old Chief's
Country].

Trans. Lore Kruger.
Berlin: Tribune, 1956.

Contents: A home for the highland cattle-- The
old chief Mshlanga-- No witchcraft for sale-- The
antheap-- Hunger

Hungary

108. ELDORÁDÓ: ELBESZÉLESÉK [Five: Short Novels].

Trans. Tibor Bartos.
Budapest: Uj Magyar Kiadó, 1956.

Contents: A home for the highland cattle-- The
other woman-- Eldorado-- The antheap-- Hunger

Italy

109. L'ERBA CANTA [The Grass Is Singing].

Trans. Maria Stella Ferrari.
Rome: Casini, 1952.

110. LA NOIA DI ESSERE MOGLIE:ROMANZO [A
Proper Marriage].

Trans. Fracesco Saba Sardi.
Milan: Feltrinelli, 1957.

111.   A CIASCUNO IL SUO DESERTO [Each His Own
       Wilderness].

       Trans. Liciano Codignola.
       Turin: Einaudi, 1963.

112.   IL TACCUINO D'ORO [The Golden Notebook].

       Trans. Maria Rivia Serini.
       Milan: Feltrinelli, 1964.

113.   COMMEDIA CON LA TIGRE [Play with a Tiger].

       Trans. Maria Rivia Serini.
       Turin: Einaudi, 1967.

Latvia

114.   BURVESTĪBA NAV PARDODAMA [stories from
       This Was the Old Chief's Country and Five].

       Trans. Z. Stava.
       Riga: Latgosizdat., 1961.

       Contents: The old chief Mshlanga--No witch-
       craft for sale--The nuisance--Little Tembi--
       'Leopard' George--The antheap--Hunger

Netherlands

115.   HET ZINGEN DE GRAS [The Grass Is Singing].

Trans. Paul van Kampen.
Amsterdam: G. W. Breughel, 1953.

116.   EEN MAN EN TWEE VROUWEN [stories from A
Man and Two Women].

Trans. P. van Vliet.
Amsterdam: J. M. Meulenhof, 1965.

   Contents: One off the short list--The sun between
   their feet--A woman on a roof--Two potters--How
   I finally lost my heart--A man and two women--A
   letter from home--Our friend Judith--Homage for
   Isaac Babel--Outside the ministry--To room nineteen

117.   PAS OP JEZELF, LIEVELING [stories from A
Man and Two Women].

Trans. P. van Vliet.
Amsterdam: J. M. Meulenhf, 1966.

   Contents: The story of two dogs--England versus
   England--Each other--Notes for a case history--
   A room--Between men--Dialogue--The new man

Norway

118.   DET SYNGER I GRESSET [The Grass is Singing].

Trans: Eli Krog.
Stavanger: Stabenfeldt, 1951.

Poland

119.   MROWISKO [Five: Short Novels].

Trans. Agnieszka Glinczanka.
Warsaw: Pánstw. Instytut Wydawn., 1956.

Contents: The antheap--Hunger--Eldorado--A
home for the highland cattle--The other woman

120.   POKOJ NR 19 [stories from A Man and Two Women].

Trans. Waclaw Niepokólczycki.
Warsaw: Pánstw. Instytut. Wydawn., 1966.

Contents: The story of two dogs--Notes for a
case history--To room nineteen

Portugal

121.   A ERVA CANTA [The Grass Is Singing].

Trans. Daniel Gonçalves.
Lisbon: Ulisseia, 1964.

Rumania

122.   CEALALTA FEMEIE [stories from Five].

Trans. Mircea Alexandrescu.
Bucharest: Editua de Stat Pentru Literatura si
Arta, 1958.

   Contents: The antheap--The other woman

Russia

123.   MURAVEJNIK ["The Antheap"].

Trans. S. Terehina and I. Manenok.
Moscow: Pravda, 1956.

124.   IMEROHI EI OLE MÜÜDAV JA TEISI JUTTE
[stories from This was the Old Chief's Country].

Trans. V. Rand.
Tallinn: Gaz.-Zurn.-izd., 1957.

   Contents: The old chief Mshlanga--'Leopard'
   George--No witchcraft for sale

125.   MARTA KVEST [Martha Quest].

Trans. T. A. Kudrjavcera.
Moscow: Izdatelstvo., 1957.

126.   POVESTI [stories from This Was the Old Chief's
Country and Five].

Trans. A. Ljubovcov *et. al.*
Moscow: Izdatelstvo, 1958.

Doris Lessing

Contents: The antheap--'Leopard' George--
Hunger

127.   NAŠ SEKRET NE PRODAETSJA [stories from
Five and This Was the Old Chief's Country].

Trans. M. Šelija.
Tiflis: Nakaduli, 1963.

Contents: No witchcraft for sale--Little Tembi--
The antheap

Spain

128.   LA COSTUMBRE DE AMAR [The Habit of Loving].

Trans. Maria Luisa Borrás.
Barcelona: Seix y Barral, 1964.

Contents: The habit of loving--The words he said--
The woman--Through the tunnel--Lucy Grange--
Pleasure--A mild attack of locusts--The witness--
Flavours of exile--Flight--The day Stalin died--
Plants and girls--Wine--He--The eye of God in
paradise

129.   CANTA LA HIERBA [The Grass Is Singing].

Trans. Jose M. Valnerde.
Barcelona: Seix y Barral, 1968.

A Checklist

Sweden

130.　GRASËT SJUNGER [The Grass Is Singing].

Trans. Gunvor Hökby and Bertil Hökby.
Stockholm: Hökerberg, 1951.

131.　FLICKAN MARTHA [Martha Quest].

Trans. Gunnar Frösell.
Stockholm: Hökerberg, 1953.

132.　DEN FEMTE SANNINGEN [The Golden Notebook].

Trans. Mårten Edlund.
Stockholm: Forum, 1964.

133.　EN MAN OCH TRÅ KRINNOR [stories from A Man
and Two Women].

Trans. Harriet Alfons and Jadwiga P. Westrup.
Stockholm: Forum, 1965.

> Contents: A man and two women--One off the
> short list--How I finally lost my heart--England
> versus England--Between men--Our friend Judith --
> Outside the ministry--The sun between their feet--
> Two potters--A letter from home--Dialogue--To
> room nineteen

134.　VANAN ATT ÄLSKA [stories from The Habit of
Loving and A Man and Two Women].

Doris Lessing

Trans. Harriet Alfons and Jadwiga P. Westrup.
Stockholm: Forum, 1966.

Contents: The habit of loving--Through the
tunnel-- Pleasure--The witness--Getting off
the altitude--He--The day Stalin died--The eye
of God in paradise--The story of two dogs--Notes
for a case history

135.   KATTER [Particularly Cats].

Trans. Harriet Alfons and Jadwiga P. Westrup.
Stockholm: Forum, 1968.

136.   MARTHA QUEST: DEL I SERIEN VALDETS
BARN [Martha Quest: Vol. I, Children of Violence].

Trans. Sonja Bergvall.
Stockholm: Trevi, 1972.

United Arab Republic

137.   AL-TĪHAW KULLUN FĪ BAYDĀ'IH [Each His
Own Wilderness].

Trans. Sa'd Zahrān.
Al-Qāhirah: al-Dār al-Qua mīyah, 1966.

II. CRITICISM OF LESSING'S WORKS

E. INTERVIEWS

138.   Ebert, Roger. Chicago SUNDAY SUN-TIMES,
       Section IV (June 8, 1969), 1, 5.

139.   Haas, Joseph. Panorama: Chicago DAILY NEWS,
       14 (June 1969), p. 4-5.

140.   Howe, Florence. NATION, 204 (March 6, 1967),
       311-313.

141.   Newquist, Roy. COUNTERPOINT. New York:
       Rand McNally, 1964, pp. 414-425.

142.   Raskin, Jonah. NEW AMERICAN REVIEW No. 8.
       New York: New American Library, 1970, pp. 169-
       179.

143.   Rubens, Robert. The Queen (London), August 21,
       1962.

Doris Lessing

144.   Terkel, Studs. Unpublished radio interviews.
       June 10, 1969; October 8, 1970.

F. BIOGRAPHY

145.   Anon. PUBLISHERS' WEEKLY, 161 (February 2, 1952), 706.

146.   Bannon, B. A. PUBLISHERS' WEEKLY, 195 (June 2, 1969), 51-54.

147.   Churchill, Caryl. TWENTIETH CENTURY, 148 (November 1960), 443-451.

148.   Walters, R., Jr. NYTBR, December 4, 1966, p. 60.

149.   Wiseman, Thomas. TIME AND TIDE, 43 (April 12, 1962), 26.

G. BIBLIOGRAPHY

150.   Anon. CONTEMPORARY AUTHORS: A BRIEF
        BIO-BIBLIOGRAPHICAL GUIDE TO CURRENT
        AUTHORS AND THEIR WORKS. Detroit: Gale,
        pp. 9-10 (1965), 285.

151.   Burkom, Selma R. "A Doris Lessing Checklist,"
        CRITIQUE, XI, 1 (1968), 69-81.

152.   Harte, Barbara and Caroline Riley, eds. 200 CON-
        TEMPORARY AUTHORS: BIO-BIBLIOGRAPHIES
        OF SELECTED LEADING WRITERS OF TODAY
        WITH CRITICAL AND PERSONAL SIDELIGHTS.
        Detroit: Gale, 1969, pp. 162-168.

153.   Ipp, Catharina. DORIS LESSING: A BIBLIOGRAPHY.
        Johannesburg: University of Witwatersrand, 1967.

H. GENERAL CRITICISM

154.   Alcorn, Noeline Elizabeth. "Vision and Nightmare: A Study of Doris Lessing's Novels." Unpublished doctoral dissertation: University of California (Irvine), 1971.

155.   Allen, Walter. THE MODERN NOVEL IN BRITAIN AND THE UNITED STATES. New York: Dutton, 1965, pp. 276-277.

156.   Brewer, Joseph. "The Anti-Hero in Contemporary Literature," IOWA ENGLISH YEARBOOK, 12 (1967), 55-60.

157.   Brewster, Dorothy. DORIS LESSING. New York: Twayne, 1965.

158.   Brooks, Ellen W. "Fragmentation and Integration: A Study of Doris Lessing's Fiction." Unpublished doctoral dissertation: New York University, 1971.

159. Burkom, Selma R. " 'Only Connect': Form and Content in the Works of Doris Lessing," CRI - TIQUE, XI, 1 (1968), 51-68.

160. --- "A Reconciliation of Opposites: A Study of the Works of Doris Lessing." Unpublished doctoral dissertation: University of Minnesota, 1970.

161. --- "Wholeness as Hieroglyph: Lessing's Typical Mode and Meaning," THE FICTION OF DORIS LESSING: PAPERS COLLECTED FOR MLA SEMINAR 46 (Winter 1971), ed. Paul Schlueter. Evansville (Indiana): University of Evansville, 1971, pp. 1-11.

162. Carey, Father Alfred Augustine. "Doris Lessing: The Search for Reality; A Study of the Major Themes in Her Novels." Unpublished doctoral dissertation: University of Wisconsin, 1965.

163. Drabble, Margaret. "Doris Lessing: Cassandra in a World under Siege," RAMPARTS, X, 8 (February 1972), 50-54.

164. Gindin, James. "Doris Lessing's Intense Commitment," POSTWAR BRITISH FICTION: NEW ACCENTS AND ATTITUDES. London: Cambridge University Press, 1962, pp. 65-86.

165.   Graustein, Gottfried. "Entwicklungstandenzen
       in Schaffen Doris Lessings," WISSENSCHAFTLICHE
       ZEITSCHRIFT DER UNIVERSITAT ROSTOCK, 12
       (1963), 529-533.

166.   Hartwig, Dorothea. "Die Widerspeigelung Afrikan-
       ischer Probleme im Werk Doris Lessings," WISSEN-
       SCHAFTLICHE ZEITSCHRIFT DER UNIVERSITAT
       ROSTOCK, 12 (1963), 87-104.

167.   Karl, Frederick. A READER'S GUIDE TO THE
       CONTEMPORARY ENGLISH NOVEL. London:
       Thames and Hudson, 1963, pp, 281-283.

168.   --- "Doris Lessing in the Sixties: the New Anatomy
       of Melancholy," CONTEMPORARY LITERATURE,
       XIII, 1 (Winter 1972), 15-33.

169.   Kauffmann, Stanley. "Literature of the Early
       Sixties," WILSON LIBRARY BULLETIN, XXXIX,
       9 (May 1965), 751-752.

170.   Marchino, Lois A. "The Search for the Self in the
       Novels of Doris Lessing," THE FICTION OF
       DORIS LESSING: PAPERS COLLECTED FOR MLA
       SEMINAR 46 (Winter 1971), ed. Paul Schleuter.
       Evansville (Indiana): University of Evansville,
       1971, pp. 1-14.

171. McDowell, Frederick P. W. "The Devious In-
     volutions of Human Character and Emotions:
     Reflections on Some Recent British Novels,"
     WISCONSIN STUDIES IN CONTEMPORARY
     LITERATURE, IV, 3 (1963), 346-350.

172. --- "The Fiction of Doris Lessing: An Interim
     View," ARIZONA QUARTERLY, XXI, 4 (Winter
     1965), 315-345.

173. --- "Recent British Fiction: Some Established
     Writers," CONTEMPORARY LITERATURE, II, 3
     (Summer 1970), 401-431.

174. Millar, John Clive. "The Contemporary South
     African Short Story in English: with Special Refer-
     ence to the Work of Nadine Gordimer, Doris Les-
     sing, Alan Patton, Jack Cope, Uys Krige and
     Dan Jacobson." Unpublished master's thesis:
     University of Cape Town, 1962.

175. Nkosi, Lewis. "Les Grandes Dames," NEW
     AFRICA, 7 (1965), 163.

176. Sachs, Joseph. "The Short Stories of Gordimer,
     Lessing and Bosman," TREK, XV, 11 (November
     1951), 15-16.

177.   Schlueter, Paul. "Doris Lessing: The Free
        Woman's Commitment," CONTEMPORARY BRIT-
        ISH NOVELISTS, ed. C. Shapiro. Carbondale:
        Southern Illinois University Press, 1965, pp.
        48-61.

178.   --- "A Study of the Major Novels of Doris Lessing."
        Unpublished doctoral dissertation: Southern Illinois
        University, 1968.

179.   Tucker, Martin. AFRICA IN MODERN LITERA-
        TURE: A SURVEY OF CONTEMPORARY WRITING
        IN ENGLISH. New York: Unger, 1967, pp. 175-183.

180.   Wellwarth, George E. THE THEATER OF PRO-
        TEST AND PARADOX: DEVELOPMENTS IN THE
        AVANT-GARDE DRAMA. New York: New York
        University Press, 1964, pp. 248-250.

I. CRITICISM OF INDIVIDUAL WORKS

THE GRASS IS SINGING

181.   Anon. KIRKUS, 18 (July 1, 1950), 366.

182.   --- NEW YORKER, 26 (September 16, 1950), 107.

183.   --- TLS, April 14, 1950, p. 225.

184.   Barkham, John. NYTBR, September 10, 1950, p. 4.

185.   Church, Richard. JOHN O'LONDON'S, March 17, 1950, p. 4.

186.   Govan, C. N. SATURDAY REVIEW, 33 (October 21, 1950), 44.

187.   Johnson, Pamela Hansford. DAILY TELEGRAPH

(London), March 14, 1950.

188.   Jones, Ernest. NATION, 171 (September 23, 1950), 273.

189.   Laski, Marghanita. SPECTATOR, 184 (March 31, 1950), 443.

190.   --- TIME, 56 (September 18, 1950), 44.

191.   Shrapnel, Norman. MANCHESTER GUARDIAN, March 17, 1950, p. 4.

192.   Spencer, Joanna. NY HERALD TRIBUNE BOOK REVIEW, September 10, 1950, p. 8.

193.   Walbridge, E. F. LIBRARY JOURNAL, 75 (September 1, 1950), 1408.

194.   White, Anatonia. NEW STATESMAN AND NATION, 39 (April 1, 1950), 378.

195.   Wyndham, Francis. OBSERVER, March 19, 1950.

THIS WAS THE OLD CHIEF'S COUNTRY: STORIES

196. Anon. BOOKLIST, 49 (September 1, 1952), 13.

197. --- OBSERVER, August 21, 1966, p. 14.

198. --- TLS, May 11, 1951, p. 289.

199. Fitzgerald, E. J. SATURDAY REVIEW, 35 (August 2, 1952), 19.

200. Laski, Marghanita. OBSERVER, April 22, 1951, p. 7.

201. Olsen, Bruce F. " 'A Sunrise on the Veld:' Analysis," INSIGHT II: ANALYSES OF MODERN BRITISH LITERATURE, eds. John V. Hagopian and Martin Dolch. Frankfurt: Hirschgraben, 1965, pp. 234-238.

202. Peden, William. NYTBR, July 13, 1952, p. 16.

203. Snow, C. P. SUNDAY TIMES (London), April 8, 1951, p. 3.

204. Spring, Howard. COUNTRY LIFE (London), April 20, 1951, p. 1225.

205.   Stallings, Sylvia. NY HERALD TRIBUNE BOOK
       REVIEW, June 22, 1952, p. 4.

206.   Street, Allen. CURRENT LITERATURE (London),
       April 1951, p. 56.

207.   Strong, L. A. G. SPECTATOR, 185 (May 4, 1951),
       598.

208.   Symons, Julian. MANCHESTER EVENING NEWS
       (England), April 12, 1951.

209.   Wintringham, Margaret. TIME AND TIDE, 32 (July
       28, 1951), 728.

MARTHA QUEST

210.   Anon. TLS, October 24, 1952, p. 689.

211.   Charques, R. D. SPECTATOR, 189 (October 31,
       1952), 580.

212.   Petersen, C. BOOKS TODAY, 3 (April 10, 1966),
       10.

FIVE: SHORT NOVELS

213. Anon. TLS, July 7, 1952, p. 457.

A PROPER MARRIAGE

214. Anon. TLS, October 22, 1954, p. 669.

215. Amis, Kingsley. SPECTATOR, 193 (October 8, 1954), 450.

216. Davenport, John. OBSERVER, September 26, 1964, p. 9.

217. Hackett, A. PUBLISHERS' WEEKLY, 190 (October 3, 1966), 90.

RETREAT TO INNOCENCE

218. Anon. TLS, April 27, 1956, p. 251.

219. Daniel, George. SPECTATOR, 96 (March 16, 1956), 354.

220.   Richardson, Maurice. NEW STATESMAN AND
       NATION, 51 (March 24, 1956), 284.

A HABIT OF LOVING

221.   Anon. BOOKLIST AND SUBSCRIPTION BOOKS
       BULLETIN, 55 (September 1, 1958), 22.

222.   --- KIRKUS, 26 (March 15, 1958), 364.

223.   --- OBSERVER, April 24, 1966, p. 22.

224.   --- TIME, 22 (July 14, 1958), 88.

225.   --- TLS, November 29, 1957, p. 717.

226.   Fuller, Roy. LONDON MAGAZINE, 5 (March
       1958), 69.

227.   Glauber, R. H. NY HERALD TRIBUNE BOOK
       REVIEW, July 13, 1958, p. 4.

228.   Gordimer, Nadine. AFRICA SOUTH, 2 (July-
       September 1958), 124.

229.   Hartley, L. P. SPECTATOR, 199 (November 22, 1957), 706.

230.   Heineman, Margot. DAILY WORKER (London), January 2, 1958.

231.   Johnson, Pamela Hansford. NEW STATESMAN, 54 (November 23, 1957), 700.

232.   Johnson, Vernon. MANCHESTER GUARDIAN, November 26, 1957, p. 4.

233.   Klein, Marcus. HUDSON REVIEW, 11 (Winter 1958-1959), 625.

234.   Michael-Jena, Ruth. WEEKLY SCOTSMAN, January 11, 1958.

235.   Montgomery, John. LIBRARY JOURNAL, 83 (July 1958), 2052.

236.   Moriarty, M. BEST SELLERS, 18 (August 1, 1958), 162.

237.   Peden, William. NYTBR, July 20, 1958, p. 4.

238.   Sullivan, Richard. Chicago SUNDAY TRIBUNE, July 13, 1958, p. 3.

239.   Symons, Julian. EVENING STANDARD (London), November 19, 1958.

GOING HOME: DRAWINGS BY PAUL HOGARTH

240.   Anon. PUBLISHERS' WEEKLY, 193 (January 29, 1968), 98.

241.   --- TLS, May 10, 1957, p. 283.

242.   Bacon, M. H. ANTIOCH REVIEW, 25 (Fall 1965), 447.

243.   Miller, C. SATURDAY REVIEW, 51 (March 23, 1968), 45.

244.   Plomer, William. NEW STATESMAN AND NATION, 53 (May 25, 1957), 680.

245.   Ross, Alan. SPECTATOR, 197 (May 31, 1957), 726.

A RIPPLE FROM THE STORM

246. Anon. TLS, October 24, 1958, p. 605.

247. Richardson, Maurice. NEW STATESMAN, 56 (October 18, 1958), 539.

EACH HIS OWN WILDERNESS

248. Brien, Alan. SPECTATOR, 200 (March 28, 1958), 389.

249. Worsley, T. C. NEW STATESMAN, 55 (March 29, 1958), 405.

IN PURSUIT OF THE ENGLISH: A DOCUMENTARY

250. Anon. BOOKLIST AND SUBSCRIPTION BOOKS BULLETIN, 57 (March 15, 1961), 447.

251. --- JOHN O'LONDON, July 7, 1960.

252. --- TIME, 77 (March 3, 1961), 62.

253.   --- TLS, July 1, 1960, p. 416.

254.   Baro, Gene. NY HERALD TRIBUNE LIVELY
        ARTS, March 19, 1961, p. 31.

255.   Bliven, Naomi. NEW YORKER, 37 (December 2,
        1961), 234.

256.   Bowers, Faubion. SATURDAY REVIEW, 44
        (March 25, 1961), 25.

257.   Bradbury, Malcolm. NYTBR, March 5, 1961, p. 4.

258.   Colimore, V. BEST SELLERS, 20 (March 15,
        1961), 477.

259.   Corbett, Hugh. BOOKS ABROAD, Spring 1961,
        p. 206.

260.   Cosman, Max. COMMONWEAL, 74 (April 14,
        1961), 86.

261.   Dangerfield, George. NATION, 192 (April 15,
        1961), 324.

262. Findlater, Richard. EVENING STANDARD (London), June 14, 1960.

263. Fraser, R. A. San Francisco CHRONICLE, March 5, 1961, p. 26.

264. Gilliatt, Penelope. SPECTATOR, 204 (May 20, 1960), 740.

265. Glick, Nathan. NEW LEADER, 44 (November 27, 1961), 29.

266. Goldsborough, Diana. TAMARACK REVIEW, 19 (Spring 1961), 101.

267. Grauel, George E. AMERICA, 104 (March 18, 1961), 796.

268. H. B. H. SPRINGFIELD REPUBLICAN, March 12, 1961, p. 4D.

269. Jones, Mervyn. OBSERVER, May 8, 1960, p. 23.

270. Lambert, G. W. SUNDAY TIMES (London), June 5, 1960, p. 16.

271.   Laski, Marghanita. NEWS CHRONICLE (London), May 11, 1960.

272.   Mair, L. P. LISTENER, 63 (May 26, 1960), 945.

273.   Mudrick, Marvin. HUDSON REVIEW, 14 (Summer 1961), 284.

274.   Potts, Paul. LONDON MAGAZINE, 7 (September 1960), 82.

275.   Prescott, Orville. NY TIMES, April 7, 1961, p. 29.

276.   Price, R. G. G. PUNCH, 239 (September 7, 1960), 357.

277.   Rosselli, John. GUARDIAN, May 12, 1960, p. 6.

278.   Ware, Jean. LIVERPOOL DAILY POST, June 1, 1960.

279.   Waterhouse, Keith. NEW STATESMAN, 59 (June 4, 1960), 832.

THE TRUTH ABOUT BILLY NEWTON

280.   Anon. NEW STATESMAN, 59 (January 23, 1960), 100.

THE GOLDEN NOTEBOOK

281.   Anon. BOOKLIST, 59 (September 1, 1962), 31.

282.   --- KIRKUS, 30 (May 1, 1962), 432.

283.   --- NEWSWEEK, 60 (July 2, 1962), 82.

284.   --- PUBLISHERS' WEEKLY, 193 (January 29, 1968), 100.

285.   --- TIME, 80 (July 13, 1962), 74.

286.   --- TLS, April 27, 1962, p. 280.

287.   --- TIMES WEEKLY REVIEW (London), April 26, 1962, p. 10.

288.   Bliven, Naomi. NEW YORKER, 39 (June 1, 1963), 114.

289.   Boman, Sylvia. NEWS-SENTINEL (Fort Wayne),
        June 30, 1962.

290.   Bowen, John. PUNCH, 242 (May 9, 1962), 733.

291.   Britten, Anne. BOOKS AND BOOKMEN, 7 (May
        1962), 53.

292.   Brooks, Jeremy. SUNDAY TIMES (London), April
        16, 1962, p. 32.

293.   Buckler, Ernest. NYTBR, July 1, 1962, p. 4.

294.   Cruttwell, Patrick. HUDSON REVIEW, 16 (Winter
        1962-1963), 591.

295.   Dolbier, Maurice. NY HERALD TRIBUNE, June
        29, 1962, p. 17.

296.   Duchene, Anne. GUARDIAN, July 8, 1962, p. 7.

297.   Emerson, Joyce. BOOKMAN, May 1962.

298.   Fruchter, Norman. STUDIES ON THE LEFT, 4
        (Spring 1964), 123.

299. Hicks, Granville. SATURDAY REVIEW, 45 (June 30, 1962), 16.

300. Hope, Francis. OBSERVER, April 15, 1962, p. 28.

301. Howe, Irving. NEW REPUBLIC, 147 (December 15, 1962), 17.

302. Kramer, H. NEW LEADER, 48 (October 25, 1965), 21.

303. Magid, Nora. COMMONWEAL, 77 (October 5, 1962), 53.

304. Matthew, Roy. LONDON MAGAZINE, 2 (June 1962), 95.

305. Mitchell, Julian. SPECTATOR, 208 (April 20, 1962), 518.

306. Moore, Harry T. BOSTON HERALD, July 1, 1962.

307. Neiswender, Rosemary. LIBRARY JOURNAL, 87 (June 15, 1961), 2399.

308.   Nordell, Roderick. CHRISTIAN SCIENTIST MONI-
        TOR, 3 (July 5, 1962), 11.

309.   Nott, Kathleen. TIME AND TIDE, 43 (April 26,
        1962), 33.

310.   Prescott, Orville. NY TIMES, June 29, 1962, p.
        25.

311.   Scannell, Vernon. LISTENER, 67 (May 3, 1962),
        785.

312.   Stone, Judy. San Francisco SUNDAY CHRONICLE,
        July 22, 1962, p. 23.

313.   Taubman, Robert. NEW STATESMAN, 63 (April 20,
        1962), 569.

314.   Toledano, Robert de. NATIONAL REVIEW, 13
        (September 25, 1962), 235.

315.   Watson, W. H. C. THE SCOTSMAN, April 21, 1962.

316.   White, Ellington. KENYON REVIEW, 24 (Autumn
        1962), 750.

A PLAY WITH A TIGER: A PLAY IN THREE ACTS

317.   Anon. ILLUSTRATED LONDON NEWS, 240 (April 7, 1962), 554.

318.   --- NEW STATESMAN, 63 (March 30, 1962), 462.

319.   --- NEW YORKER, 40 (January 9, 1965), 86.

320.   --- SPECTATOR, 208 (March 30, 1962), 398.

A MAN AND TWO WOMEN

321.   Anon. NEWSWEEK, 62 (October 14, 1963), 118.

322.   --- SATURDAY REVIEW, 48 (November 20, 1965), 40.

323.   --- TLS, October 18, 1963, p. 821.

324.   --- TIMES WEEKLY REVIEW (London), October 24, 1963, p. 13.

325.   Auchincloss, Eve. NY REVIEW OF BOOKS, 1

(October 17, 1963), 5.

326.   Deane, Peter. BOOKWEEK, October 13, 1963,
        p. 16.

327.   Dolbier, Maurice. NY HERALD TRIBUNE, October
        14, 1963, p. 23.

328.   Gindin, James. SATURDAY REVIEW, 46 (November 23, 1963), 42.

329.   --- TIME, 82 (October 18, 1963), 68.

330.   Hamilton, A. BOOKS AND BOOKMEN, 10 (April
        1965), 55.

331.   Howard, R. PARTISAN REVIEW, 31 (Winter 1964),
        117.

332.   Howes, B. MASSACHUSETTS REVIEW, 5 (Spring
        1964), 583.

333.   Kauffmann, Stanley. NYTBR, October 13, 1964,
        p. 4.

334. Mudrick, Marvin. HUDSON REVIEW, 17 (Spring 1964), 110.

335. Pickrel, Paul. HARPER'S, 227 (November 1963), 132.

336. Pollock, Venetia. PUNCH, 244 (November 13, 1963), 722.

337. Schott, Webster. NATION, 197 (December 14, 1963), 419.

338. Stiles, Patricia. LIBRARY JOURNAL, 88 (November 15, 1963), 4396.

339. Sullivan, Richard. Chicago SUNDAY TRIBUNE MAGAZINE OF BOOKS, November 3, 1963, p. 3.

340. Taubman, Robert. NEW STATESMAN, 66 (November 8, 1963), 653.

341. Wardle, Irving. OBSERVER, October 6, 1963, p. 25.

AFRICAN STORIES

342.   Anon. BOOKLIST, 62 (December 1, 1965), 354.

343.   --- CHOICE, 2 (December 1965), 684.

344.   --- KIRKUS, 33 (September 1, 1965), 939.

345.   --- NEWSWEEK, 66 (October 18, 1965), 128.

346.   --- SATURDAY REVIEW, 49 (September 24, 1966), 40.

347.   --- TLS, April 23, 1964, p. 329.

348.   Brophy, B. NEW STATESMAN, 68 (July 3, 1964), 22.

349.   Brown, Edward R. SATURDAY REVIEW, 48 (October 23, 1966), 67.

350.   Casey, F. CHRISTIAN SCIENCE MONITOR, 58 (January 6, 1966), 11.

351.   Cassity, T. KENYON REVIEW, 28 (March 1966), 279.

352. Edelstein, J. M. COMMONWEAL, 83 (January 28, 1966), 514.

353. Ellmann, Mary. NATION, 202 (January 17, 1966), 78.

354. Fleischer, L. PUBLISHERS' WEEKLY, 189 (June 6, 1966), 233.

355. Foster, Paul. TABLET, 218 (April 24, 1964), 470.

356. Garis, Robert. PARTISAN REVIEW, 33 (Spring 1966), 302.

357. Green, Martin. BOOK WEEK, 3 (November 21, 1965), 22.

358. Kramer, Hilton. NEW LEADER, 48 (October 25, 1965), 21.

359. Levine, N. SPECTATOR, 212 (April 17, 1964), 522.

360. Moutafakis, G. J. SOCIAL EDUCATION, 30 (March 1966), 207.

361. Mudrick, Marvin. HUDSON REVIEW, 19 (Summer 1966), 305.

362. Peterson, V. BOOKS TODAY, 3 (April 3, 1966), 12.

363. Ready, W. LIBRARY JOURNAL, 90 (December 15, 1966), 5416.

364. Scott, J. D. NYTBR, November 7, 1965, p. 4.

365. Stille, Elizabeth. REPORTER, 34 (January 13, 1966), 53.

LANDLOCKED

366. Anon. TLS, June 24, 1965, p. 533.

367. Barker, Paul. NEW SOCIETY, June 24, 1965, p. 27.

368. Bradbury, Malcolm. PUNCH, 249 (July 14, 1965), 66.

369.   Byrom, Bill. SPECTATOR, 214 (June 25, 1965), 826.

370.   Coleman, J. OBSERVER, June 20, 1965, p. 66.

371.   Corbett, E. AMERICA, 114 (April 2, 1965), 450.

372.   Taubman, Robert. NEW STATESMAN, 70 (July 2, 1965), 19.

373.   Tisdall, J. BOOKS AND BOOKMEN, 10 (July 1965), 26.

374.   Wood, F. T. ENGLISH STUDIES, August 1966, p. 315.

WINTER IN JULY

375.   Anon. OBSERVER, August 21, 1966, p. 14.

PARTICULARLY CATS

376.   Anon. BOOKLIST, 64 (September 1, 1967), 29.

377.   --- BOOKS AND BOOKMEN, 13 (December 1967), 50.

378.   --- KIRKUS, 35 (March 15, 1967), 389.

379.   --- PUBLISHERS' WEEKLY, 191 (March 13, 1967), 57.

380.   Cook, Roderick. HARPER'S , 235 (July 1967), 95.

381.   Jacobson, E. BOOKS TODAY, 4 (April 30, 1967), 15.

382.   Radosta, J. S. NY TIMES, May 6, 1967, p. 29.

383.   Willis, K. T. LIBRARY JOURNAL, 92 (April 15, 1967), 1635.

THE FOUR-GATED CITY

384.   Anon. CHOICE, 6 (November 1969), 1222.

385.   --- NEW YORKER, 45 (June 14, 1969), 114.

386.   --- TIME, 94 (July 25, 1969), 75.

387.   --- TLS, July 3, 1969, p. 720.

388.   Cole, B. SPECTATOR, 222 (July 5, 1969), 18.

389.   Corbett, E. P. J. AMERICA, 161 (September 13, 1969), 171.

390.   Cruttwell, Patrick. BOOK WORLD, May 25, 1969, p. 8.

391.   Daly, D. ATLANTIC MONTHLY, 224 (July 1969), 101.

392.   Dalton, Elizabeth. COMMENTARY, 49 (January 1970), 85.

393.   Ellmann, Mary. NYTBR, May 18, 1969, p. 4.

394.   Enright, D. J. NY REVIEW OF BOOKS, 13 (July 31, 1969), 22.

395.   Grant, Annette. NEWSWEEK, 73 (May 26, 1969), 117.

396.   Hardwick, Elizabeth. VOGUE, 154 (July 1969), 50.

397.   Hill, B. AMERICA, 121 (November 29, 1969), 531.

398.   Hill, W. B. BEST SELLERS, 29 (July 1, 1969), 141.

399.   Howe, Florence. NATION, 209 (August 11, 1969), 116.

400.   Kuehl, Linda. COMMONWEAL, 90 (June 20, 1969), 394.

401.   Leonard, J. NY TIMES, May 15, 1969, p. 45.

402.   Lydon, Sue. RAMPARTS, 8 (January 1970), 48.

403.   Millar, G. LISTENER, 82 (July 3, 1969), 21.

404.   Oates, Joyce Carol. SATURDAY REVIEW, 52 (May 17, 1969), 48.

405.   --- HUDSON REVIEW, 22 (Autumn 1969), 531.

406.   Raban, J. LONDON MAGAZINE, 9 (September 1969), 111.

407.   Rascoe, Judith. CHRISTIAN SCIENCE MONITOR, 10 (July 3, 1969), 9.

408.   Schlueter, Paul. CHRISTIAN CENTURY, 87 (January 28, 1970), 121.

409.   Shorter, Kingsley. NEW LEADER, 52 (July 7, 1969), 13.

410.   Thompson, J. HARPER'S, 239 (September 1969), 122.

411.   Tindall, G. NEW STATESMAN, 77 (July 4, 1969), 19.

412.   Wadsworth, C. E. LIBRARY JOURNAL, 94 (June 15, 1969), 2486.

BRIEFING FOR A DESCENT INTO HELL

413.   Anon. NEWSWEEK, 77 (April 12, 1971), 118.

414.   DeMott, Benjamine. SATURDAY REVIEW, 54 (March 13, 1971), 25.

415.   Didion, Joan. NYTBR, March 14, 1971, p. 1.

416.   Langley, Lee. GUARDIAN, April 14, 1971, p. 8.

417.   Lask, Thomas. NY TIMES, March 10, 1971, p. 41.

418.   Maddocks, Melvin. TIME, 97 (March 8, 1971), 80.

419.   --- CHRISTIAN SCIENCE MONITOR, 12 (March 18, 1971), 11.

420.   Sale, Roger. NY REVIEW OF BOOKS, 16 (May 6, 1971), 13.

421.   West, Paul. BOOK WORLD, February 28, 1971, p. 1.

CHILDREN OF VIOLENCE

422.   Anon. CHOICE, 1 (February 1965), 555.

423.   --- CHOICE, 3 (June 1966), 307.

424.   --- KIRKUS, 33 (December 1, 1965), 205.

425.   --- TIME, 84 (November 20, 1964), 94.

426.   Allen, Walter. NYTBR, November 15, 1964, p. 5.

427.   --- NEWSWEEK, 64 (December 7, 1964), 106.

428.   --- NEW YORKER, 40 (January 30, 1965), 122.

429.   --- NYTBR, April 3, 1966, p. 41.

430.   Ashley, Leonard R. N. "Children of Violence as
        a 'Golden Notebook:' The Writing of Doris Lessing."
        THE FICTION OF DORIS LESSING: PAPERS COL-
        LECTED FOR MLA SEMINAR 46 (Winter 1971),
        ed. Paul Schlueter. Evansville, Indiana: Univer-
        sity of Evansville, 1971, pp. 1-15.

431.   Bannon, B. A. PUBLISHERS' WEEKLY, 89 (Feb-
        ruary 7, 1966), 91.

432.   Bergonzi, Bernard. NY REVIEW OF BOOKS, 4
        (February 11, 1965), 12.

433.   Carroll, J. M. LIBRARY JOURNAL, 91 (January
        15, 1966), 278.

434.   Corbett, E. P. J. AMERICA, 112 (January 2,
        1965), 21.

435.   --- AMERICA, 114 (April 2, 1966), 450.

436.   Dalton, Elizabeth. KENYON REVIEW, 27 (Summer
        1965), 572.

437.   Davenport, Guy. NATIONAL REVIEW, 17 (Feb-
        ruary 23, 1965), 155.

438.   Deinstag, Eleanor. NEW REPUBLIC, 152 (January
        9, 1965), 19.

439.   Fremont-Smith, E. NY TIMES, December 17, 1964,
        p. 43.

440.   Graver, Laurence. NEW REPUBLIC, 154 (April
        2, 1966), 27.

441.   Harvey, D. D. SOUTHERN REVIEW, 5 (Winter
        1969), 259.

A Checklist

.   Hicks, Granville. SATURDAY REVIEW, 47 (November 14, 1964), 33.

443.   --- SATURDAY REVIEW, 49 (April 2, 1966), 31.

444.   Howe, Florence. NATION, 200 (January 11, 1965), 34.

445.   --- NATION, 202 (June 13, 1966), 716.

446.   Neiswender, Rosemary. LIBRARY JOURNAL, 89 (December 15, 1964), 4932.

447.   Owen, Roger. COMMENTARY, 39 (April 1965), 79.

448.   Perry, Eleanor. BOOK WEEK, 2 (November 15, 1964), 3.

449.   Peterson, V. BOOKS TODAY, 2 (January 3, 1965), 5.

450.   --- BOOKS TODAY, 3 (April 3, 1966), 12.

451.   Smith, Diane S."A Thematic Study of Doris Lessing's Children of Violence." Unpublished doctoral

dissertation. Chicago: Loyola University, 1971.

452.   --- "Ant Imagery as Thematic Device in the Children of Violence Series," THE FICTION OF DORIS
LESSING: PAPERS COLLECTED FOR MLA SEM-
INAR 46 (Winter 1971), ed. Paul Schlueter. Evansville, Indiana: University of Evansville, 1971, pp.
1-14.

453.   Walsh, J. NATIONAL OBSERVER, 5 (April 18,
1966), 20.

454.   Yanitelli, V. R. BEST SELLERS, 24 (December
15, 1964), 377.

455.   --- BEST SELLERS, 26 (April 15, 1966), 33.

456.   Young, Marguerite. BOOK WEEK, 3 (April 3, 1966),
5.

INDEX

Note: All titles of Lessing's works are in capitals.

85